250 Writing Prompts

VISUAL AND VERBAL SPARKS TO IGNITE YOUR STORY

A You Can Write It Production

You Can Write It Books
Portland, Oregon

To the writer inside of us all!

Wouldn't it be nice if you wrote something so good it was quoted in the epigraph of a book?

–THE PERSON WHO COMPILED THESE PROMPTS AND PREPARED THIS BOOK

Contents

Operating Instructions

You can never have too many writing prompts. In a good writing group, you have a good, respectful group of folks with unique voices and projects. It's even better if you have snacks too. In the <u>Amherst Writers and Artists</u>-style writing groups I've participated in, the facilitator has always had a grab bag of prompts to keep people writing. And some snacks. That winning combination led to countless hours of happy writing, self-discovery, friendships, and of course, wonderful stories. I can't help you with the snacks here, but I *can* help you with the prompts.

As a writer, I've been searching for sparks to get started for a long time. There are tons of books and websites with writing prompts, some of which are free. However, I've seldom found any that I found inspiring. Books that purport to have hundreds of writing prompts have disappointed me when the "prompts" were really just random questions posed to the reader. They were great guides for, say, speed dating, and maybe they worked for other people, but I didn't find them useful for getting a flash of inspiration or for getting inside a character's head. Other guides were visually hard to use: My eye would end up falling on another prompt, and I would get distracted. Still other guides only used the same kind of prompts over and over, like direct questions or specific situations. Maybe these worked for some people, but they didn't work for me.

So I decided to be the change I wanted to see in the world, and I developed a writing prompt book that contains writing prompts that I, at least, would actually use. These prompts are grouped in a way that moves them from structured and specific to more abstract.

Most of these prompts are verbal, and some are visual (I'd love to have included more visual prompts, but the file got unwieldy). I'm confident that at least some of them will speak to you, and help you unlock your incredible stories! There are more stories and ideas than there are atoms in the universe. That is a scientific fact that I just made up! See, fiction is fun! I wanted to help deepen the grab bag for those writing facilitators or just those looking to write on their own at home, or anywhere else. (Don't write and drive, though).

There are six sections to this book, each of which has a different type of prompt. The first consists of **situations or premises** that can get you started on a story or scene. These are more structured and specific prompts that can help if you are blocked, or if you just like more specifics before diving in. If the premise isn't enough, most of the prompts in this section are followed by some questions that your story could answer if you feel like it or if it helps you fill in the details. You can also ignore the questions.

The second section offers **short vignettes about characters** whose stories you should tell. I have tried to keep them gender-neutral so you can make the characters yours as much as possible. These might help if you have a character-driven approach to writing.

The third section offers snippets of **conversations and dialogues or monologues**. These sentences or phrases can be interpreted however you want.

The fourth section focuses on **you**, or at least, **the "you" that you are writing as**. This might be good for memoir or journal writing, or just for getting inside the voice and backstory of a character. You can use these in ESL classes, for public speaking, or any other situation that might benefit from some writing fodder.

The fifth section is designed to get you thinking about **writing in different styles**. Each prompt will challenge you to try to get out of your comfort zone with language and storytelling. While you can do whatever you please with each prompt, the first set is designed to be writing exercises while the other set in this chapter adds a stylistic challenge to other prompts in this book.

They say a picture is worth a thousand words, so the sixth and final section is **visual**. It consists of images from old photographs or other ephemeral documents from my personal collection (i.e., the overflowing boxes of estate and yard sale finds that my spouse wants me to get rid of). There are also public domain images that I have attributed as thoroughly as possible whenever possible. I have used these prompts with English language learners and children, as well as with native speakers and adults. Sometimes an image is a refreshing way to return to an idea, or to generate a new one!

As for formatting, I've tried to make the writing prompt book I wish I had (and now I do!). I have kept the print large so that the prompts can be read easily if, say, you're sharing the book and writing with a buddy. I've added some blank spaces in between prompts so it is easier to keep track of where you are, and harder to be overwhelmed and distracted. Of course, if you end up distracted in a serendipitous way, go with it.

There is one rule: There are no rules. **Break the rules. Just not that one.** Use the premise, write about its opposite, reject it, make it a major part of what you write, barely mention it, whatever. Some of the characters may only be passersby in your own characters' lives; some of the premises may be at the core of a story or just a moment. It's up to you. But I hope you give these ideas the loving homes that they deserve within your incredible stories! Let me know how it goes: Get in touch on YouCanWriteIt.com.

As the Amherst Writers and Artists method puts it, and as I strongly believe, *you have a powerful and unique voice.* Your stories deserve to be told. I truly hope this book helps you generate those stories. I can't wait to hear about them!

Ideas and Tips

Use this book however you find it useful.

Here are some ideas if you aren't sure what that would look like for you:

Roll a die or use a <u>random number generator</u> to pick a prompt, or scroll / flip through the book until you find something that speaks to you. Or you can go through each prompt in the book in order, or backwards, or beginning with a section that intrigues you. If you're on an e-reader, search (CRTL +F) for a particular word.

Set a timer. A good amount of time to start with is fifteen or twenty minutes. Write for the whole time the timer is going – no excuses and no distractions! Don't pause, don't reread what you wrote, and most important of all, don't revise! Just write. It's much easier to revise than it is to remember something you wrote and second-guessed yourself about. And speaking of revision, **don't revise until after the timer is done. While the timer is going, writing should go in only one direction – on the page (or screen)!**

Don't feel like you have to quote the entire prompt, or any of it. It's a starting point, but it does not have to be at the beginning of what you write, or indeed, in it at all. You also don't have to take it literally. You can change any of the details in it. If it gets you thinking about something completely different, then great! **The most important thing is that you write.**

Don't like the prompt? Obviously you can change it, discarding any parts you don't like. Just as you might answer the question you wish you had been asked, you can also write the prompt you wish you had been prompted with!

Finally, have fun.

Premises & Places

E ach of these prompts evokes a specific situation. Interpret each one however you see fit – there's no right or wrong way to read them.

Important note: All personal pronouns here are used for the sake of simplicity. Feel free to switch them up or use non-binary pronouns. And of course, when it says "you," it can mean you, the person who is reading this book or you, as in a first-person narrator / character, or anything / one else that inspires you.

1. It's the perfect party for the end of the world. Who's throwing it? What is there to eat or drink? Are there costumes? How does it end (and begin)?

2. Two former lovers meet after decades apart. At last, neither is married to or in a relationship with anyone else – but yet they can never be together. Why? Who are they, and have they changed?

3. You find a 1912 penny under the stairs and want to tell its life story. Where has it been in its life? What has it seen? Who has bought things with it, and what have they bought?

4. A small group of friends run a struggling website dedicated to finding the Next Big Thing. Just when they are about to give up, they find it where they least expect it. What is it? What makes it different? Where do they find it and how do they use it?

5. You're stuck in traffic on the highway. You haven't moved in an hour. You need the bathroom – *badly*. What do you do? What happens? Why is the traffic backed up?

6. S/he went to her twentieth high school reunion against her best judgment, only to find that s/he did not recognize a single person there – and they did not recognize her. Even the high school mascot seemed different. Why is s/he having these memory lapses? Who are the people? What happened to the school?

7. I work at a coffee shop. Every day, my favorite customer comes in and orders the same thing: A soy cappuccino with an extra shot, and tips me well. But today, s/he didn't show. Not only do I want his / her tip, but I'm worried. Should I go look for the customer? What do you think I'll find?

8. It's a small, sleepy town, and the police blotter in the paper carefully reports on every crime: Stolen lawn ornaments, double parking, abandoned notebooks. Until one day, a new police chief takes over. Determined to improve the town, s/he changes the police department's priorities. Six months later, what does the police blotter section look like? What crimes are reported? Are suspects caught? Do you get a different impression of the town?

9. S/He sits at the fresh gravesite, trying not to cry as s/he fingers the tattered top hat. It belonged to his uncle (aunt). Even though s/he is too sad to stand up, s/he knows s/he will spend the rest of his life trying to fulfill his / her uncle's wishes. Who was the uncle? What were the wishes? What will the nephew (niece) do? Will s/he succeed?

10. Your boss has called you to his/her office and has not told you why. You are standing in front of their desk, trying to seem calm, but not bored. Your boss is fidgeting nervously behind their desk, avoiding eye contact. What happens next?

11.   Three neighbors of very different backgrounds are convinced that there is something sinister going on in one house in the neighborhood. Why? What is going on? Why do they think something is off? What do they do about it? What are the dynamics like among these three neighbors?

12.   Someone's following you through the city. You have no idea who they are or why, but you see them everywhere you go. Who are they? Why are they following you...or are they?

13.   Your teenage kid has taken the last clean drinking glass to their room again, so you go in there to get it – again. The glass is on their desk, next to what looks like a journal or diary. Unable to withstand your curiosity, you glance at it and learn something that shocks you. What is it? What does it tell you about the teenager? How does your reaction show what kind of parent you are – and is it different from the kind of parent you thought you would be?

14.   A seasoned New Yorker who's seen everything is stuck on the 7 train (again), when suddenly their eyes go wide: Something they could never have imagined has caught their eyes. What is it?

15.   A man is waking up from a coma. As he opens his eyes and takes in the ICU, he slowly begins to realize nothing will ever be the same. What happened? What has changed? How will it affect him?

16.   You have to give a big presentation at work. You should have been preparing for months – but you hate your job and have never been able to work on it. You are standing behind the podium right now, and your boss, and many others, are expecting brilliance. What do you do? (What have you been doing instead of working on the presentation?)

17.   I worked hard all through college and even grad school to be a drug and alcohol counselor. I did everything I was supposed to do, but now that I'm looking for jobs, I've learned that you can't really get work in this field if you've never had substance abuse problems. What should I do?

18.   You agreed to watch your friend's toddler for an afternoon. But s/he won't stop crying. What do you do? How do you try to make him/ her stop?

19.   While waiting at the checkout line in the grocery store, you recognize the face of the person behind you: It's a missing person. Posters with their age-progressed face are all over the city you used to live in. You are totally sure it is that person. What do you do? Where has the person been? Does this person want to be found?

20.   You're a college professor meeting with one of your most enthusiastic students who has come to your office hours. You have to break it to this extremely enthusiastic, but untalented student, that not only did they fail their most recent exam, but that you

cannot write them a recommendation for the scholarship they are applying for. What do you say? What does the student do?

21.   You're standing on the ugliest carpet in the world. What does it look or smell like? How does it feel to stand on it, barefoot or not? What makes it ugly?

22.   You have just broken up with your significant other, and are driving away from their home when you get pulled over. What happens next?

23.   Just one shoe lies on the side of the road. How'd it get there and where's its mate?

24.   A fifty-two-year-old (wo)man has finally achieved all of their goals, hopes, and dreams. Now what?

25.   You got invited to what you thought was a party, but it's actually a sales pitch for a multilevel marketing company. How do you escape (or do you)?

26.   It's the world's best cookie recipe, and the grandmotherly woman who bakes it is utterly determined to keep it a secret. No matter what. Even though rival bakers are always trying to steal

the recipe. What does she do to keep the secret? How do others try to get it? What's the recipe, anyway? Are the cookies even that good?

27. Someone receives their neighbor's package by mistake. It is oddly shaped and makes mysterious noises when they shake it. What's in it? Why? Do they try to return it?

28. A young child is seriously ill. His or her younger sibling is devastated not just by the illness, but by their parents' almost complete attention to the other sibling. How does the younger brother / sister act out? How does it affect their relationship with their sibling and parents?

29. The O'Ligarck Corporation is about to cut down the oldest tree in the state so they can build a new office building. Many people are highly opposed to this move. What happens?

30. You wake up hungover after a fun night and discover that your wallet is missing. You retrace your steps and stops the night before, trying to find your wallet. Where have you been? What have you done?

31. The person sitting next to you on the plane is quiet and has avoided eye contact. They seem sad and anxious. Do you try to ask what's wrong? How do you interact with this person for the remaining six hours of the flight? ....By the way, your in-flight entertainment system isn't working, either. The airline is very sorry

about that and will give you 50,000 miles as compensation when you land. Until then, you have to contend with your seatmate.

32. An old classmate of yours has recently hit it big...by creating a TV show where the main character, an unlikable and cringe-inducing anti-hero, is you. What do you do?

33. A young writer is so paralyzed by fear of unintentional plagiarism that he or she second-guesses all their ideas. Why are they so anxious? What are the brilliant ideas they're convinced are derivative?

34. It'll be a full moon tonight, and the local Werewolves Union is preparing some PR statements to fight stereotypes of lycanthropy. What do they write and what does that meeting look like?

35. Tonight is the opening night of a highly anticipated play. The stakes are high: It's supposed to re-launch the career of a "has-been" actor. The critics are excited, the buzz is loud, the seats are sold out. Finally, the curtain comes up and...(What happens next?)?

36. After years of waiting, a wo/man is finally a grandmother (Father)! She (He) flies across the country to meet the new grandchild...and is speechless because the baby is, to put it kindly, not cute. What happens? Does it impact their relationships with their in-laws?

37. All dogs go to heaven; it's a fact. But could this cause any problems? Are there issues with dogfights in heaven, and good boy;

(girls) not picking up after themselves? What happens if an angel steps in heavenly dog waste? Is heaven full of dog hair? (Does the author of this book maybe think about this a little too much?)

38.   At an airport bar, a solo traveler waits (and waits) for their flight. S/he observes an obnoxious patron who has clearly never flown before and who has clearly never been in a bar, either; this person tries to rip off the bartender by not paying. What happens next?

39.   The empty, grassy lot at the corner of the neighborhood is where all the kids play. Friendships are forged, alliances and toys are broken, life lessons are learned. Describe a strong friendship that forms here and how it is tested.

40.   In 1959, a murdered Jane Doe was found in the city. She has never been identified and has become the stuff of local legend and true crime television shows. One day, an elderly-sounding person calls the police department. "I know who Jane Doe was," s/he begins....

41.   Imagine a horrible, dystopian world. What's wrong with it? Can it be fixed? Are its problems natural (e.g., the result of natural disasters) or man-made (e.g., the result of society), or something else? Is it fictional or inevitable in our "real" world?

42.   In 1918, the Spanish Flu pandemic was estimated to kill up to 5% of the world's population and infected around 500 million people. Tell the story of someone who survived, but almost did not.

43.   The musician's biggest fan has spent years following his (her) every move, curating a website, collecting bootlegs, and running an online fan club. Now, s/he'll finally get to meet their hero. However, the meeting is disappointing. How does the musician fail to live up to these expectations? How does the fan react?

44.   Who's living in the run-down looking car that parks in your neighborhood at night? You know, the one filled with what looks like garbage and paper so you can't see in the windows. What's their story, and what happens when your nosy HOA president neighbor knocks on their passenger-side window?

45.   Hansel and Gretel is a pretty boring and upsetting fairy tale when you get right down to it: Full of messages about healthy eating, bringing maps with you when you go to unfamiliar places, and of course, the misogyny that dominates so many fairy tales. I bet you can write a better version. Go for it.

46.   After the death of their mother, three adult siblings get tested to see if they have the gene for the type of cancer that killed her. What are the results of the tests? How do the results amplify longstanding sibling rivalries and tensions?

47.   Someone who has been unathletic and sedentary their entire life decides to make a dramatic change to be healthier. What do they do? How does this work out for them? How does it affect their sense of self?

48.   Thanks to an enormous breakthrough in medicine, life expectancy is now 150 years. How does this change society, relationships, families, and the economy?

49. Describe a terrible first (and last) date.

50. All of the writing prompts are boring, cheesy, or seem like they're for kids. You roll your eyes, knock the book off the table (or hurl your reading device across the room), and come up with your own writing prompt – and it sparks the greatest story you have ever read. Tell me about it.

Characters in search of stories

I 'd like to introduce you to some people. Who are they? Heck if I know! You tell me. All I know is, they each have unique stories, and are in need of someone to tell those stories. You know more about them than I do, so choose one of these people and be the author they need! Adopt one today!

Note: All pronouns here are used for the sake of simplicity. Feel free to switch them up or use non-binary pronouns, obviously. Although some of these characters may sound specifically modern or Western, please consider that they might not live in our contemporary era or culture, or even in our world.

1. An elderly man or woman who wants to unburden themselves of lifelong secrets...all of which are *very* boring

2. A perfectly ordinary librarian with sensible shoes who is going to change her life radically today

3. A small child who pretends to be terrified of everything

4. A beloved aging rock star who lives in fear that people will find out his / her twin has written all their lyrics

5. A middle-aged amateur genealogist who is frustrated to find out that his / her family is *exactly* who they thought they were

6. Someone who is completely obsessed with true crime and murder mysteries

7. A bored young adult who infiltrates a local group they have no business being in – and finds out it is not what they thought

8. Every student's least favorite teacher who just might have a good reason for being so tough, demanding, and mean

9. A stay-at-home mother, the kind who puts Martha Stewart to shame with her incredible cooking, beautiful home, and apparent perfection

10. The guy who was once valedictorian of his high school class, but who can now barely hold a job at a convenience store

11. A panhandling drug user on the corner who desperately wants to get clean and reconnect with their family

12. A successful young doctor who is disillusioned and burned out with their career choice

13. Someone who has just been (mis)diagnosed with a terminal illness

14. A professional online poker player who can't break free of a toxic ex

15. A bartender at a dive bar at the edge of the city

16. A guy (gal) who is determined to start a world-famous podcaster, but who has a terrible voice and a stigmatizing accent

17. A veteran with PTSD

18.   A vegan who drives to distant towns and enjoys steak dinners alone

19.   The blue-collar twenty-something struggling to keep a spending and debt problem secret from his or her wealthy friends

20.   A middle-aged married wo/man who is beginning to question all of the beliefs of their upbringing

21.   A young adult whose mother blogged their entire infancy and early childhood

22.   A misanthrope who works at a funeral home

23.   Someone who just got a shocking and life-changing diagnosis, including a diagnosis of a disease being in remission, or of the patient not having a disease

24.   The last resident of a future ghost town

25.   A sensitive writer who is new to town and unsure of what they want here: A sequel, another chapter, a new book entirely?

26.   Someone with a pet pig (the big kind, not pot-bellied!) who walks it down the street every day at 2 PM

27.   An older woman who never had children, married, learned to drive, or flown on a plane

28.   A university professor who can't stop thinking about a certain student

29.   A middle-aged father whose teenage son/ daughter has run away, tearing the family apart

30.   A twentysomething whose startup, which is about to go bankrupt, employs all of their friends

31.   A kidnapping victim returning to their family

32.   A nurse working double shifts at a hospice

33.   A renowned restaurateur who is lax about washing his or her hands

34.   The long-married couple who decide that things are too perfect so they should seek out affairs

35.   A "mad" scientist

36.   The parent who cyberbullies the son / daughter of their child's classmate

37.   A TSA screener at a tiny airport where nothing ever happens

38.   A convenience store owner who sacrificed everything to buy this franchise

39.   Someone starting a revolution, whether they know it or not.

40.   A perennial candidate for a local office whose wacky ideas are a punchline around the city

41.   Someone who ended up at the wrong New Year's Eve party

42.   A serial grad student who has started seven different master's degrees, and completed two of them

43.   The "other woman" (or man) who is fully aware that she is the other woman (or man)

44.   The owners of the Bates Motel. No, not *that* one. Yeah, they get that a lot.

45.   A brilliant physics student recovering from a traumatic brain injury (TBI)

46. The mother of a Millennial living in her basement who is going to be kicked out of the house and forced to live on his/ her own, today.

47. An electrician who wants to retire early by investing in penny stocks

48. A twenty-something who has just spent the past year taking care of his / her mother, who succumbed to cancer yesterday

49. The RA (resident advisor) of a college dorm where the rules are repeatedly violated

50. The person who writes a book of 250 writing prompts

Overheard dialogues, monologues, and other people's texts

I f you read something out of context, it can take on new meaning. For that reason, this section is a veritable set of verbal microscope slides: Quick lines pulled out of their context, ready for you to clone into your own Frankenstein's Monster of prose.

Or something like that.

Each prompt consists of exactly one spoken line. Your job is to put these decontextualized lines back into context. In other words, clone them and let them loose into the (or into *a*) world. You do not even need to directly quote them.

1. "If only I had known it really *would* be the last happy night of my life."

2. "I'm not into all that sports stuff. I just really like violence."

3. "No idea. The box just said: Pens that don't work."

4. "He's been failing upwards his whole life."

5. "You don't understand. It's real to me."

6. "Are you *sure* you don't want to go to the hospital?"

7. "Sorry. I must have gotten your dander up."

8. "And that's how I became a folk hero."

9. "That's the third time you've taken a so-called social media sabbatical in the past month."

10.   "Tell me something interesting.

11.   "Stop fiddling with your watch and look at me."

12.   "Gimme some sugar."

13.   "It only happens in odd-numbered years."

14.   "Why'd I stop? I suddenly smelled Yorkshire pudding!"

15.   "Oh yes, you *can* handle the truth."

16.   "My last hero died today."

17.   "That's impossible. There are thousands of dollars in that account."

18.   "Who takes the last wilting lettuce from a salad bar?"

19.   "And there, sitting next to me at the bar, was none other than Jimmy Carter."

20.   "Hello. I'm calling because you have a 100% satisfaction guarantee, but I was only 97% satisfied."

21.   "Hang up and call me back from a pay phone."

22.   "I'm jealous of babies. They don't have to follow any rules."

23. "I'm sorry, that flight has been canceled."

24. "Mom? Who's that guy in the backyard?"

25. "I absolutely *promise* that you don't want me on the jury."

26. "No, that is not my suitcase. You must be looking for someone else."

27. "I never thought I would see you again!"

28. "If you signed up for the History of Everything class then yes, you are in the right place. Otherwise, may I persuade you to stay?"

29. "Dad, did it ever occur to you that maybe the problem isn't other people mumbling, but the fact that you've needed hearing aids since Bush was president?"

30. "I found it under the blackberry brambles."

31. "We're not going to be paying that today."

32. "Nope, never heard of her."

33. "You might want to try the plus-size section."

34. "It breaks my heart to do this."

35. "You need to stop living like a college student."

36. "I'm telling you, I just spent an hour looking. I can't find my car anywhere in this garage."

37. "*That?!* You really hold a grudge."

38. "It's Erica with a C. Short for *America*."

39. "I did count. We're three sheep short."

40. "I cannot refill this prescription for you until next month."

41. "Do you wanna take this outside? Because we can take this outside."

42. "The Toccata Fugue in D-minor – I'd recognize it anywhere."

43. "Officer, I think it' more than whiplash."

44. "A B+? But I *need* an A. Please, is there anything I can do?"

45. "Time to wrap it up. We have to say goodbye now."

46. "I've done enough free work for you."

47. "Drink more water. Your lips are chapped."

48. "It wasn't a big deal at the time, but it bodes poorly for the future. You need to think about whether you really want to be here."

49. "I can't understand you. For once, can you just talk like a normal person?"

50. "Excuse me, sir, but I need to see your ID before you can enter that area."

The Story of You

There are several ways to use this section (and I am sure you can think of others!). One would be to use these as journal prompts. Another could be to answer in the voice of a character you're working with (hopefully you adopted at least one character from the earlier section). Thinking through some of these questions in their voice can be a great way to understand their motives. A third could be to use these questions to get to know other people, though I'm more of an expert on writing than on social engineering.

I guess these could make cocktail parties either more or less awkward, depending on the parties (and the cocktails) involved.

1. What is your earliest memory? Pay particular attention to the sensory details.

2. How was your day today?

3. What is your deep (or shallow), dark secret? Do others think it is dark? Why do you keep it a secret?

4. What is the change you want to see in the world, and what is the change you have been or continue to be in the world?

5. We all have scars. What is your scar story? (Is the one you tell people different from the real story?)

6. Do you have siblings? If so, how many? Are you the eldest, middle, youngest, or only? What immediately comes to mind when you think about your siblings?

7. What five songs are the hit singles in the soundtrack to your life, and why?

8. What is your idea of a perfect day?

9. What beliefs or ideas have you had that turned out to be false? How did you learn this?

10.   When you were younger, who had the biggest individual impact on your life? Was this impact ultimately positive or negative, and why?

11.   What are your five biggest values (e.g., integrity, creativity, etc.), and why? How do you apply them, or how and when have you failed to apply them, in your life?

12.   Are you similar to your parents, grandparents, or siblings? If so, how? If not, what makes you different?

13.   When you were in school, what kind of student were you? What subjects did you love, and which did you dread? What did your teachers think of you?

14.   Describe your sense of humor. What do you find funny? Do others share this view?

15. Describe one food (or meal) that evokes a strong emotional reaction in you. What is it? Why does it affect you in this way?

16. What does the Table of Contents for your life look like?

17. Who is your exact opposite? What do they look like, how do they dress, what do they do for a living?

18. Describe something you witnessed that you have never been able to understand.

19. Which books and movies have had a major impact on your life, and why?

20. Write about a time when you thought you were in real danger. What happened? How did you get through it?

21. How would you describe your personal style?

22. Do you believe more in destiny or in free will? Discuss.

23. How do you feel about animals? Have you had any special pets or other animals in your life? Describe them.

24. When people ask where you are "from," what is your answer and why? Sometimes it's not as simple as how long you have lived somewhere.

25. Which bad habit do you think is the worst? Who do you know who has or does it? Why does it bother you?

26. What accomplishment are you proudest of and why?

27. What three dates in the past year have been most significant to you and why?

28. What is the sickest (or worst injured) you have ever been? What happened and how are you doing now?

29. What is your dream vacation? Tell me about the destination, means of travel, activities, companions, etc.

30. Were you ever bullied? Or were you a bully? Did you witness bullying?

31.   What have you done recently to make the world a better place?

32.   What have you done recently that might have made the world a *worse* place? Did you do it on purpose?

33.   Have you ever been pulled over? What happened?

34.   If you ever run for public office, which of your youthful indiscretions will your opponents bring up? How will you respond?

35.   Describe the worst haircut you've ever had.

36.   How do you feel about gardening? As a hobby, that is, not a metaphor.

37.   What is the worst advice you have ever given someone? Why was it the worst?

38.   What is the worst advice you have ever been given? Why was it the worst?

39. Has a piece of art ever brought you to tears? (Any form of art: Music, film, painting, etc.) Describe the work and your feelings.

40. Who was your *second* love?

41. What happens after we die? How would you explain this to a child?

42. Do you have any tattoos? If so, tell me what they mean to you.

43. What do you think makes someone a leader? Are you a leader or more of a follower? Why?

44. What word or phrase do you use a little too often? Why do you use it so much?

45. When you were younger, what did you want to do with your life? Is it what you are doing now?

46. Have you ever gone to the emergency room? Were you there as a patient or bringing someone? What was wrong and how was it resolved?

47.   What is the strangest dream you have ever had?

48.   If you had to choose, which would it be: Video games or card games? Why? If just choosing either makes you grimace, why?

49.   Not enough people write thank-you cards anymore. Who in your life deserves one from you, and why? Maybe you should write it.

50.   What do you wish someone would ask you?

SECTION FIVE

"Exercices de Style"

I, your humble narrator, your font of writing prompts, once became mildly Internet famous for writing an essay that had no verbs in it. It was about how people should not use verbs. This was way back in the pre-viral days, and nearly twenty years later, that silly essay I wrote while bored in study hall remains the high-water mark for success in my life (ouch). Every now and then someone emails me about it. All this to say that writing something in a new way can change your life in unexpected ways.

Anyway, the wonderful little book _Exercices de Style (Exercises in Style)_ by Raymond Queneau is a book that retells the same minor incident 99 times in ninety-nine different ways. That book definitely inspired this section. It is always good to get out of your comfort zone. If you always write in the first person and in the past tense, maybe some stylistic exercises can help you. I'm not asking you to rewrite a story ninety-nine different ways, but if you experiment with _how_ to write, you will doubtless discover something new!

There are two sub-sections here. The first consists of exercises and ideas, and the second involves picking other prompts in the book and then applying a stylistic challenge. Of course, feel free to break the rules. Feel free to write your own rules (Oh hey, it looks like someone actually got **_251_** writing prompts for the price of 250! Tell all your friends!).

Exercises

1. Describe your favorite flavor of ice cream (or some other delicious dessert), but do not use any adjectives.

2. Write your shopping list as a sonnet.

3. Describe a day at the beach, but use only ONE sense (taste, smell, touch, hear, or see) to do so.

4. Write a Terms of Service contract between a dog and its human.

5. Write a Terms of Service contract between a cat and its human.

6. Write a course syllabus (including weekly readings and assignments) for a love affair that ended badly.

7. Describe a boring day at the office, but in the style of a celebrity gossip blog / social media account.

8. Write an extended metaphor for a dinner party.

9. Write a song about a hangnail.

10. Analyze why people like something you hate (e.g., a band, a trend, a sports team) and write in the style of an academic paper.

11. Write about a historical person you respect and admire, but describe them in a way that would make the reader hate him or her.

12. Think of something that most people find rather disgusting (bodily functions / fluids, mold, etc.) and then describe it in a way that makes it beautiful.

Pick any prompt BUT...

1. Write only in the future tense.

2. Write in only one (long) sentence.

3. Write in the style of a lurid tabloid newspaper, complete with a screaming headline.

4. Write like an angry YouTube commenter.

5. Write so simply that a five-year-old could understand it.

5. Write in the style of the voiceover for a movie trailer.

7. Write in an archaic, Shakespearean style.

3. Write it as a list of items.

9. Write with NO dialogue, and focus on imagery. Let the word-images speak for the story.

10. Write from the perspective of an alien entity that has no experience with or context of earth.

11. Write no sentence with more than **five words.**

12. Write it like an instruction manual with a series of steps.

13. Make the narrator someone very different from both the main character and yourself: Pick a (second, if applicable) character from the character chapter and make that person the narrator.

SECTION SIX

Ephemera and images

T hey say a picture is worth a thousand words, so by my calculation, you should be able to get a good 25,000 out of these decontextualized images. Go get 'em!

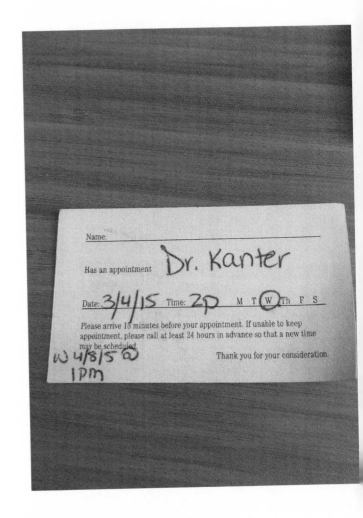

ZEUSTEMPLET I ATHEN

1

NORTH LAKE—LOOKING NORTHWEST.

2

4

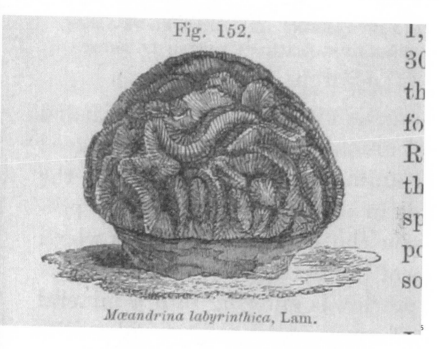

Fig. 152.

Mæandrina labyrinthica, Lam.

Fall 244.   Abb. 167. Der Würgengel (Buntstift).   29×40

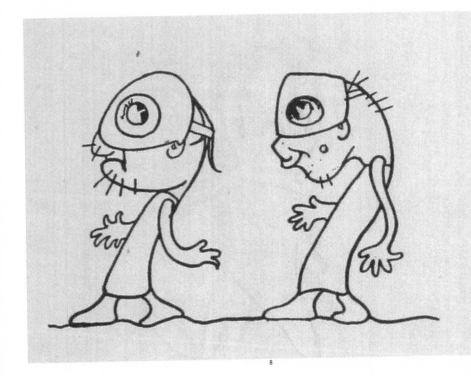

8

Under the Red Gums.

Notes

[1] Image taken from page 15 of 'Verdens Storbyer. | Translated from 'Les Capitales du monde.' | Paa Dansk af P. Nansen. Med 322 Afbildninger.' Courtesy of The British Library's public domain image library.

[2] Image from Wilcox, W.D. "Camping in the Canadian Rockies ... With ... a sketch of the early explorations ... With ... illustrations, etc." New York: 1896. P. 231. Courtesy of The British Library's public domain image library.

[3] James, R. "The Fashionable Lady; or, Harlequin's Opera. In the manner of a rehearsal, etc. [With musical notes.] London: 1730. P. 92. Courtesy of The British Library's public domain image library.

[4] Marsh, Richard. "The Beetle: A mystery, etc." Skeffington & Son, London: 1897. P. 201. Courtesy of The British Library's public domain image library.

[5] Unknown artist. Courtesy of The British Library's public domain image library.

[6] Unknown artist. Courtesy of *The Public Domain Review*.

[7] Basevi, George. *Bird's-eye view of the Soane Family Tomb* (1816). Courtesy of *The Public Domain Review*.

[8] Artist unknown. From *Lilliput Lyrics*. J. Lane: London, 1899. Courtesy of The British Library's public domain image library

[9] Campbell, A.J. Ca. 1895. Courtesy of *The Public Domain Review*.

[10] Photographer unknown. *From In the Shadow of Sinai: a story of travel and research from 1895 to 1897.* Courtesy of The British Library's public domain image library. Figure in image is purported to be Monseigneur Porphyrios, Archbishop of Mount Sinai.

ABOUT THE AUTHOR

YOUR PHOTO, NAME AND BIOGRAPHY HERE

(Are you seriously reading an "About the Author" page in a book designed to get **_you_** writing? Write it yourself! ....Oh hey now, looks like someone got *two hundred and fifty*-**TWO** prompts for the price of 250! Please leave a nice review on Amazon, gossip about us on social media, and check out more writing prompts from <u>You Can Write It Books</u>!)

Made in the USA
Middletown, DE
12 July 2020

12517809R00047